THE BUSHMEN

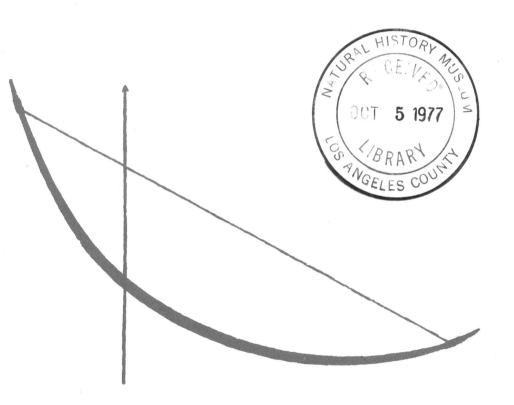

Published by the Trustees of the
SOUTH AFRICAN MUSEUM
Cape Town
1976

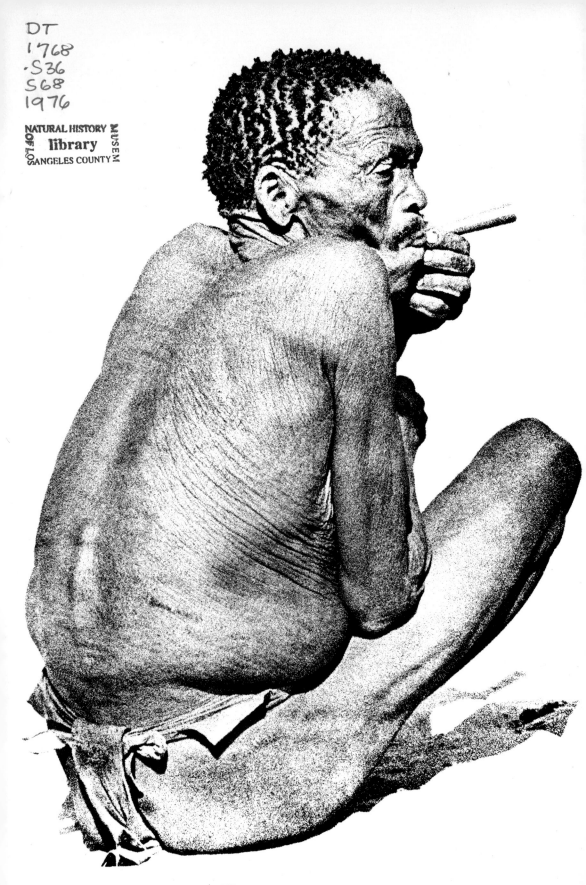

THE BUSHMEN: HUNTERS AND GATHERERS OF SOUTHERN AFRICA

The Bushmen are direct descendants of people of the Later Stone Age in southern Africa. They were, until very recently, one of the few remaining peoples of the world who have avoided the main stream of civilization and maintained the way of life that was common to mankind before the domestication of plants and animals. Traditionally they lived by hunting game and gathering food and other necessities. They were thus entirely dependent on their environment and their knowledge of how best to exploit it.

It is not yet known where the Bushmen originated nor when they first appeared in southern Africa, but human bones found at several sites suggest that they were present at least 10 000 years ago. With the Hottentots, who are also descended from Later Stone Age people, they form a racial group generally known as Khoisan, from Khoikhoin (the Hottentot term for themselves) and San (the Hottentot term for Bushman). The Bushman did not and do not have an overall name for themselves. The name 'Bosjesman' (Bushman) was given by the early Dutch settlers to distinguish those who lived entirely on the resources of the 'bush' from those who were pastoralists, and whom they called Hottentots. These names 'Bushman' and 'Hottentot', which have survived in common speech, are thus cultural terms and indicate only the way of life.

The Bushmen are genetically related to the negroes of Africa but the relationship is an ancient one, and the Bushmen now look very unlike most other African people. They are generally short, slender people with noticeably small hands and feet. Their skin, which varies in colour from light to medium yellowish brown is very dry and soft in texture and tends to wrinkle early in life. They have little body hair and the hair of the head is fine and curls so tightly that it often gives the appearance of tufts on the scalp. Both sexes have a tendency to hollow back and some women, when they reach childbearing age, accumulate a great deal of fat on the buttocks (steatopygia) and thighs (steatomeria). The shape of the face, with high cheek-bones and widely spaced, oblique and almond-shaped eyes often produces considerable beauty in young people.

ARCHAEOLOGICAL RECORD

Archaeological excavations in South Africa are yielding a great deal of evidence concerning the lives and habits of the ancestors of the Bushmen. Stone tools, man's basic implements in Africa for two or three million years, had been greatly refined by Later Stone Age times. Bone, wood and other plant materials were also used in the manufacture of equipment. Small delicately-made stone artefacts were probably used to arm arrows. Some have actually been found fastened to one end of wooden sticks. These people used the bow and arrow, and fishing and fowling were part of the hunter's activities. Bone tools included arrowheads and awls for piercing skins to make holes for the thread when sewing clothing or other articles of skin. Apart from such utilitarian implements the people found time to prepare delicate ornaments of ostrich egg-shell, sea-shells, bone and plant seeds. Necklaces, pendants and bangles have been found around the necks and limbs of excavated skeletons. Ochre in shades of red, or occasionally yellow, was ground and used as a cosmetic and was also used to anoint the dead before burial.

The food remains found at archaeological sites give an insight into the diet of the Bushmen's Stone Age ancestors. Roots and corms were evidently staple foods in inland areas. Game, mainly small buck and smaller animals such as rock-rabbit, dune mole-rats and tortoises, were also important items of diet. Coastal sites reveal masses of sea-shell and fish remains, and the presence of fish gorges and sinkers clearly indicates that line fishing was successfully practised.

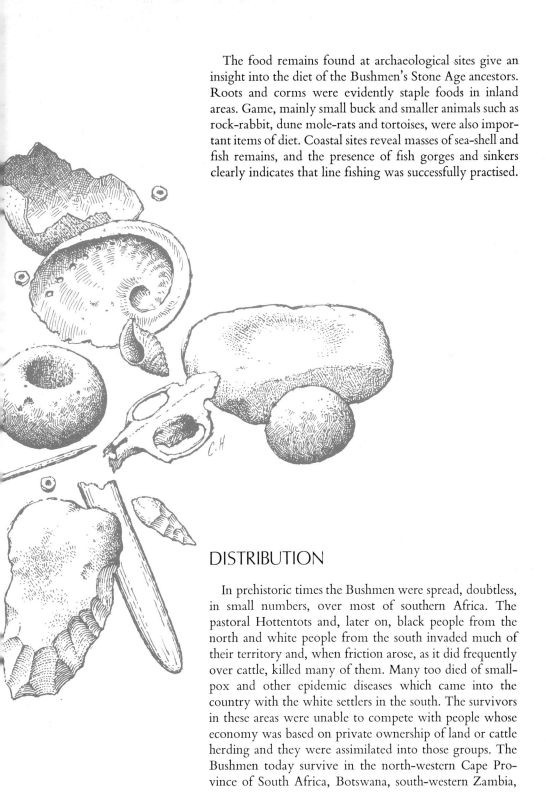

DISTRIBUTION

In prehistoric times the Bushmen were spread, doubtless, in small numbers, over most of southern Africa. The pastoral Hottentots and, later on, black people from the north and white people from the south invaded much of their territory and, when friction arose, as it did frequently over cattle, killed many of them. Many too died of small-pox and other epidemic diseases which came into the country with the white settlers in the south. The survivors in these areas were unable to compete with people whose economy was based on private ownership of land or cattle herding and they were assimilated into those groups. The Bushmen today survive in the north-western Cape Province of South Africa, Botswana, south-western Zambia,

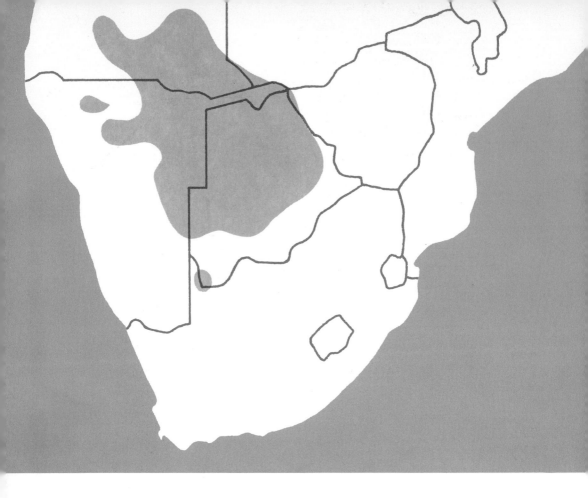

South West Africa and southern Angola—an area centered on the Kalahari Desert. It is estimated that there are 50 to 60 000 Bushmen living there today, but it is a fast diminishing minority, perhaps less than 10 per cent, that follows the old nomadic life. Although comparatively little is known of the historical Bushmen, their culture and way of life seem to have differed only in local detail from that of the living Kalahari Bushmen, who are well known from recent anthropological studies. The relationship between various major groups has not been fully established. One factor common to all is that their speech is characterized by clicks. At least four separate Bushmen languages have been recognized, however, and in addition, a very large number of people in the Kalahari, accepted as Bushmen because of their way of life, speak dialects of a Hottentot language. The description given in this brochure is of the traditional culture, as observed in the Kalahari, with some indication of the changes that have taken place.

PRESENT ENVIRONMENT

The Kalahari is not true desert. Its vegetation is a mixture of grass and a varying density of woodland on a base of sand or calcareous deposit. It has a long dry autumn and winter, with rains in spring and summer averaging in different areas from 130 mm to 650 mm (5 to 26 inches) a year. When the rainy season is normal water is preserved in pans and permanent or semi-permanent springs, and the Kalahari supports many edible plants and fruits and a large animal population. In periods of drought, however, food and water are scarce and hardship and hunger face people who themselves grow no food and own no livestock.

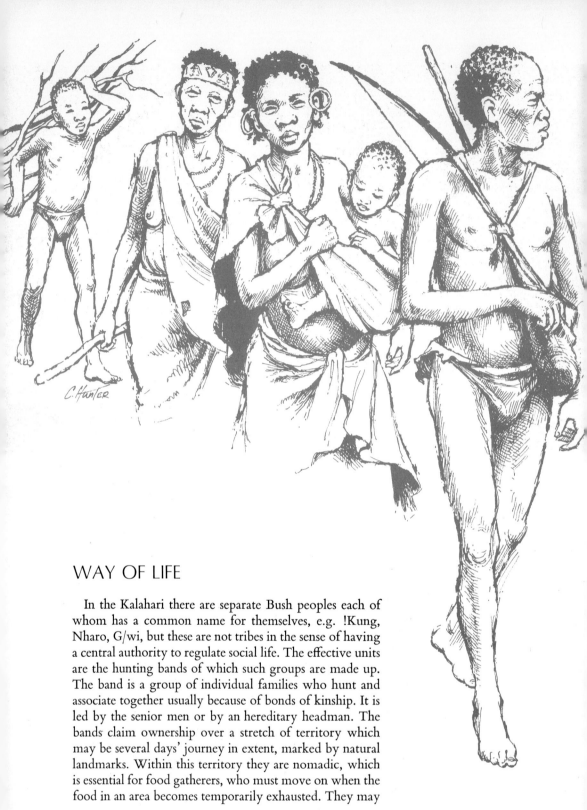

C. Hunter

WAY OF LIFE

In the Kalahari there are separate Bush peoples each of whom has a common name for themselves, e.g. !Kung, Nharo, G/wi, but these are not tribes in the sense of having a central authority to regulate social life. The effective units are the hunting bands of which such groups are made up. The band is a group of individual families who hunt and associate together usually because of bonds of kinship. It is led by the senior men or by an hereditary headman. The bands claim ownership over a stretch of territory which may be several days' journey in extent, marked by natural landmarks. Within this territory they are nomadic, which is essential for food gatherers, who must move on when the food in an area becomes temporarily exhausted. They may

even have a set route marked by waterholes, and along which they move back and forth. They follow the movements of game and have developed great skill in tracking and hunting. Through their primary dependence on plant foods, however, they have also a special knowledge of the veld and of the seasonal appearance of edible plants, and they know where water persists longest in the dry season. If the seasons are good, this need not be as hard a life as it sounds and in some areas food is sufficiently abundant for real security of life to be enjoyed. In others drought makes it difficult for people to survive. It is then that the band splits into individual families who move about on their own, searching for food.

9

SHELTER

When the bands or individual families are on the move, following game and vegetation, the women erect for shelter small roofless semicircular screens with grass bound on the outside, or even more simply may tie a few bushes together as a windbreak. During and after the rainy season, however, the bands settle in the vicinity of water but not near enough to frighten game away. Then the women build rather more substantial huts by planting branches and saplings in half to three-quarters of a circle, bending them over to meet at the top and form a frame about 1,5 metres high and about the same in diameter. The frame is filled in with brushwood and thatched with grass, and the opening can be moved according to the direction of the wind. Some people place the huts in a circle facing an open area. Others do not place them in any specific way, and there is no village form. But groups of kin will have their huts together. The floor of the hut or shelter is usually covered with grass for comfort. Huts or shelters are used only by their owners and only for sleeping, sheltering from the rain or storing their few belongings. Fires for warmth and for cooking are made in front of the huts and daily activities take place outside.

OCCUPATIONS

Hunting, gathering of food and firewood and cooking
and eating, although they are the primary occupations, do
not necessarily take up the whole of every day. There is
plenty of time left for the practice of crafts, for talking,
telling stories and playing games, for visiting each other,
sometimes at considerable distance, and for other recrea-
tions.

HUNTING

The men are the hunters and hunting is not merely a means of obtaining food but a prestige occupation by which a man proves himself as a man. A particularly successful hunter is a person of consequence in the band. Boys practise shooting with a small bow and shoot beetles and other small creatures until they are old enough to go out with the men. The weapons are the short wooden bow and poisoned arrows, the wooden club and the spear. The arrows are carried in a quiver made of skin, or of the bark of an *Acacia* root. All the weapons plus other tools, possibly in a second smaller quiver, are carried slung over the shoulder in a skin hunting-bag, which is big enough to carry small animals killed, a water-flask or other things collected on the way. Rope snares are used to trap birds and small animals, and springhares are dragged out of their burrows by means of hooks attached to long sticks.

Bushmen are skilled in the stalking of game and camouflage may be used to enable the hunter to approach without arousing suspicion—the head or the whole skin of an animal may be worn, or a leafy branch may be held up. Other devices are to copy the gait of the animal or to crawl along the ground. The effective range of the bow is about 25 metres, so these devices are necessary.

The most remarkable item of the hunting equipment is the arrow, which is in two separate parts—the head, made up of the point and foreshaft, and the light reed shaft which is notched at the butt, but not feathered. Each part bears a mark of ownership. The poison is put well behind the piercing surface of the head for fear of accident to human beings. This type of arrow allows the head to remain in the flesh of the animal if the shaft is pulled off during the victim's flight through the bushes. This gives the poison, on which the fragile arrow relies for its effectiveness, time to take effect. The poison is obtained from various substances—but in the Kalahari the grub of a beetle, which is a nerve poison, is used. It is not very fast-acting and the shot animal may have to be followed for many hours. After a successful hunt the meat is shared among the group, according to firmly established conventions, but the prerogative of sharing it out belongs to the man whose arrow killed the animal.

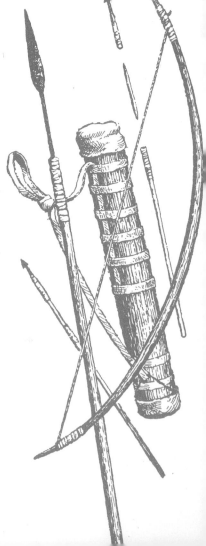

GATHERING

Although meat is considered a most desirable food, its availability is unpredictable. The basis of Bushman diet is, therefore, the more readily obtainable plant food—seeds, berries, roots, bulbs, fruits—which are collected by the women.

Honey is a luxury collected by men from certain bees' nests over which the band claims rights. This may entail the climbing of trees such as the baobab with the aid of wooden pegs inserted in the trunk.

The implement used for digging roots is a pointed digging-stick of hard wood. This is adequate for the mainly sandy conditions of present-day Bushman terrain, but in very hard ground a horn might be fixed over the point. The food that is gathered is carried home in skin bags or may be tucked into the skin cloak of the gatherer, next to the baby. Women also gather firewood. Tiny children remain at home with an older person who has been left in charge, but from the age of about 7 little girls go out with their mothers and learn to help with the gathering. Some-

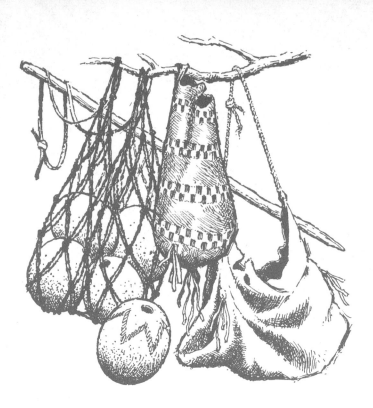

times they are able to gather enough for the family for more than one day, but going out to gather food and fire-wood is part of the normal daily routine. In certain seasons when, for example, nuts are ripe, an expedition of three or four days may be made to gather a good supply.

Water is a precious commodity often difficult to obtain in the Kalahari and rights over certain waterholes are vested in each band. Ostrich egg-shells are used as flasks for carrying and storing water. A hole is made in one end or in the side and is plugged with a grass stopper. The flasks may be filled from a pool or by sucking the water up through a reed inserted through the sand into underground water. A similar reed may be used to suck small quantities of water that has gathered in the fork of a tree. In the more arid areas a number of ostrich egg-shell flasks might be stored at a strategic spot for future use.

In the dry season, however, people may depend for their liquid requirements mainly and in some cases entirely on juicy plants, especially the *tsamma* melon (*Citrullus vulgaris*) or the blood or the moisture squeezed from the contents of the rumen of an animal that has been killed.

18

HOUSEHOLD EQUIPMENT

As befits people who are frequently on the move and
have to carry their belongings, the Bushmen have few
household goods, and set little store by the accumulation of
possessions. Men carry their goods in a skin bag slung on a
stout stick over the shoulder, and women tuck them into
the pouch made by tying a thong round the cloak at the
waist. In addition, strong nets made of thick strands of
sinew are used, especially for carrying the ostrich egg-shell
water-flasks.

A pair of stones is used for cracking nuts or crushing
various foods and also for grinding coloured ochres or
vegetable materials used as cosmetics. A pestle and a small
wooden mortar, cut out of a solid block, are used for break-
ing up harder substances. Some people fix a stone into the
bottom of the mortar. Bone or wooden blades or a knife
are used for slicing melons or fleshy bulbs, or the digging-
stick itself may serve this purpose.

Meat and items such as termites' eggs, nuts and melon seeds are roasted in the fire and scraped out of the ash with a sharpened stick. A basketwork sieve is made by some groups, to sift the ash out of such foods. Meat may be boiled too, but much of the plant food is eaten raw. To serve food tortoise-shells of different sizes may be used, or wooden bowls and ladles. Cooking and food utensils show possibly the greatest contact with other peoples. Wooden bowls and earthen pots have long been obtained from black neighbours and today metal and plastic containers are used almost everywhere.

The traditional method of making fire was with two sticks. Heat is produced by drilling a hard stick between the hands into a depression in a soft stick held by the feet, with soft grass as tinder. This equipment has been succeeded in turn by flint and tinder-boxes, matches and cigarette lighters, in that order, but all four methods are still in use today.

CLOTHING AND ORNAMENT

Clothing is made from the dressed skin of wild animals. The traditional dress for men is a roughly three-pointed loincloth, one point of which passes between the legs and is tucked into the tie-string at the back. A cloak is worn in cold weather and some men wear a fur cap. Women wear a small apron or sometimes two, and a skirt which reaches just below the knees at the back, but is shorter in front and shaped so that the apron may show.

The woman's cloak is passed under the left arm and knotted on the right shoulder. It is worn not only for warmth, but when tied round the waist it becomes a pouch for carrying home food. It is also used as a sling for carrying a baby, unless a specially shaped smaller skin is used for this purpose. Many ornaments are worn on the head, but now-adays older women are inclined to wear a cloth covering.

Sandals are sometimes worn by both sexes. In some of the sandy areas the men wear special hunting sandals which have a pointed toe curled downwards so as to grip the sand when running.

For many years now the trend has been towards the wearing of articles of modern clothing.

Bushwomen, particularly, are very fond of ornaments, and even new-born babies usually wear circlets of beads round ankles, wrists and neck. Natural objects, such as pieces of root, or reed, seeds and horns are used, but the

most important of the traditional ornaments of the Bushmen are composed of small discs of the shell of ostrich eggs. These discs are strung as necklaces or girdles, threaded into a narrow fabric for head-ornaments, or sewn on to clothing, especially on to women's aprons. Nowadays modern glass beads are taking their place and other modern objects are used, as well as metal bangles and beads traded from neighbouring metal-working people.

The ornamented shell of a small tortoise is hung round the neck or attached to the cloak or waist. It contains a powder of sweet-smelling herbs which is applied to the body with a small soft skin. Young women paint their faces and often coat their hair with powdered red ochre or powdered red wood mixed with animal fat.

Both sexes, but especially women, have tattoo marks made by rubbing ash into cuts. For women they are purely ornamental and are made on the face, thighs and buttocks. Men have cicatrization marks made on the forehead at the time of their initiation into manhood, tattoo marks on the face to indicate success in hunting and purely ornamental tattoo marks especially on the thighs and buttocks.

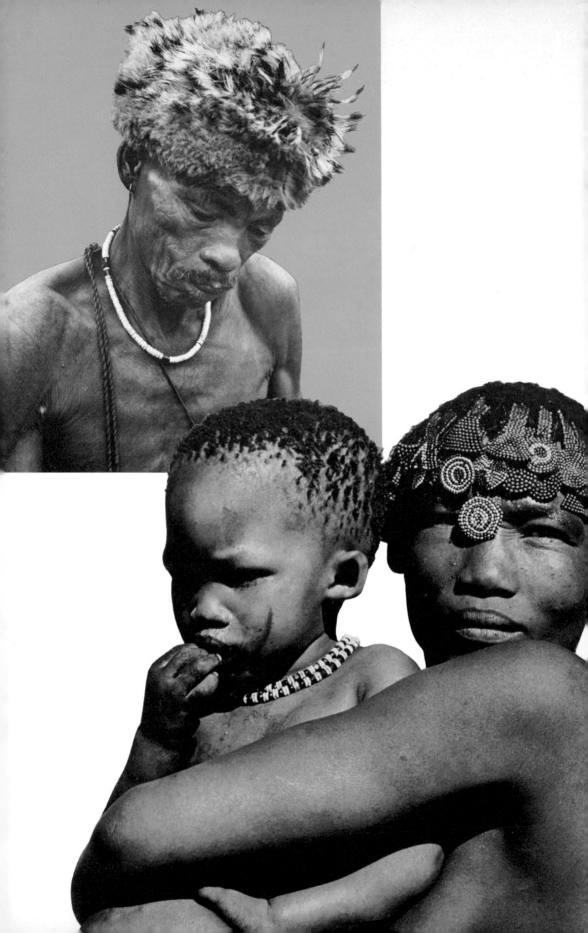

CRAFTS

There are no specialist craftsmen. Men and women make things for their own use or sometimes for exchange. This is a sociable activity which gives plenty of opportunity for conversation.

Men dress skins and make clothing and bags for various purposes and every man is responsible for providing these for his immediate family; they make weapons, tools and wooden utensils, as well as rope, string and thread from vegetable fibre or sinew. They also do all metalwork.

Wooden items made are food mortars, small poison-mortars, digging-sticks and clubs, bow staves and handles for tools. The metal which is used is obtained by trade, heated in the fire and hammered into shape with a stone. Rope is made by separating the fibres of a succulent plant, *Sanseveria,* and rolling them on the thigh into two-ply cord. The dried back sinew of animals is similarly rolled into the strong string of which carrying nets are made. Thinner strands of sinew are rolled into thread for sewing or for threading beads.

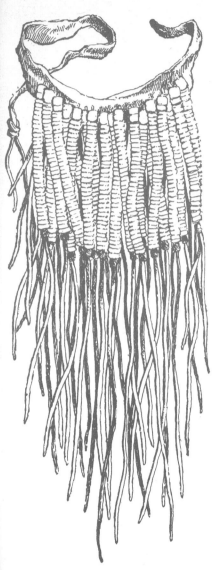

Women make all ornaments, and ornament and mend clothing. Their special craft is the making of ostrich egg-shell beads. Small pieces of the shell are roughly rounded by biting or tapping with a horn, or nowadays a piece of metal, using a stone as an anvil. A hole is drilled through the centre and the discs are strung on a thread of twisted sinew until taut and then rounded and rubbed smooth with a friable stone. These beads are made into ornaments or used to ornament clothing. In some places a whole apron is sometimes made of a fabric of ostrich egg-shell beads. Today their place has been taken to a large extent by glass trade beads.

TRADE

Long strings of ostrich egg-shell beads are a traditional medium of trade with non-Bushman groups. Unworked skins, horns, ostrich feathers, wildebeest (gnu) or gemsbok tails, and porcupine quills are also traded with black neighbours either for tobacco or metal or latterly, where there are stores, are sold for money. Several types of object, especially ornaments and bows and arrows, are now being made for the curio trade.

Among the Bushmen themselves trade or barter is replaced by the interchange of gifts, which also cements good social relationships. This is not to say that there is no idea of the values of different things, but a gift will be offered to someone who is known to want that particular article and who has something that the donor wants. Certain people or places are known to be good sources of certain things. The donor may not be successful on every occasion, but things even out in the end. This is an extension of the Bushman practice of sharing, and of having a minimum of individual possessions. An important characteristic of Bushman life is the reciprocal sharing of food and possessions. Not only is this socially acceptable, but it is an insurance against need.

RECREATION

The Bushmen are inveterate smokers, and this is the reason why tobacco is one of the main items for which goods are exchanged. Smoking is a sociable occupation and the pipe is passed round from one to another.

Story-telling is another group activity—the members of the audience will participate either by repeating a phrase like a chorus or by putting in contributions of their own. There is an extensive mythology in which supernatural creatures are featured.

Music and dancing are much enjoyed. The true Bushman instruments are the bow, the whistle and the dancing rattle. A tune may be struck with an arrow on the string of a hunting bow, but some bows are specially made for music. The mouth, the chest, a melon shell or, nowadays an old tin serve as resonators. Rattles of moth cocoons with stones or seeds inserted and strung on a fibre cord are tied round the legs to accentuate the stamping rhythm of the dance. Other instruments, as for example a type of harp and a thumb piano, have been adopted from time to time from neighbouring people.

Musical instruments are played solo, but women in particular sing as a group, in harmony, and clap a rhythm.

Dancing usually takes place at night and round the fire. The women sing and clap an accompaniment while the men dance a stamping step in a circle round them. Often they impersonate animals. Sometimes women will join in the dance.

Children and young people have many games, some of which have a singing accompaniment.

RELIGIOUS BELIEFS, MAGIC AND MEDICINE

Dancing is not only a recreation, but is often inspired by the spiritual life. Belief in spiritual beings is common to all Bushmen. Animals, celestial bodies and phenomena such as rain have been personified as supernatural beings whose activities are related in the rich mythology. Details of belief differ from group to group, but the general belief is that the world was created by a supreme being and that nature and events are controlled by supernatural beings, some good, some evil. Attempts to influence these spirits take the form less of propitiatory practices towards the good than of active steps to eradicate the evil, in which case religion merges into magic, or, when sickness is the evil, into medicine. For example, in some dances men go into a trance during which they draw into themselves the evil from the affected person and later have it expelled from them by those who, by massage and other means, bring them out of the trance.

In addition to the dances there are other magical-medical practices—the wearing of amulets and charms, the rubbing of certain substances into cuts in the skin, either to cure the affected part or to bring good luck, the drawing out of the sickness by sucking the affected spot, or by bleeding it with a cupping horn.

The course of events is foretold by throwing divining tablets of wood, calabash rind or leather. A notable instrument of magic is the tiny magic arrow set—a bundle of blunt arrows of grass-stem and horn, a bow of horn and a small leather quiver. These arrows can do no physical harm, as they are neither sharp nor poisoned, but they can produce good or bad magical results by being shot either against the clothing of a person or even into the direction of the thing that it is desired to influence.

ART

The artistic expression of the contemporary Bushmen is confined to the decoration of objects of use. But the mountain regions of southern Africa and the inland plateau do contain the richest known occurrence of rock-art in the world. Much of it is the work of prehistoric or historic Bushmen who were known still to paint or engrave the rocks in the nineteenth century.

The two types of art, engraving and painting, occur mainly in different areas, though there are a few instances where they overlap. The engravings were made on the dolerite boulders of the inland plateau of South Africa. The paintings were done on the walls of sandstone, granite or limestone rock-shelters or large boulders of the mountainous area.

The engravings were incised or pecked with a stone tool. Many are simple outlines but in some the bodily form and differences in colour of an animal are shown by pecking within the outline. The standard of work varies. A great deal of it is rough, but some is very fine, and different

styles are to be seen in different areas. The most common
subjects are large single animals such as elephants, giraffe
and various antelopes and geometric designs. Human
figures are rare. There is no certainty about the age of the
engravings nor that the artists were all Bushmen.

The paintings also show a variety of styles. They vary
from monochrome outlines and silhouettes to exquisitely
shaded polychrome figures, and they range from single
individuals to large and animated groups. There are few
plants but every type of local animal and some birds, fish
and insects are shown as well as geometrical figures,
mythical creatures and human beings. The colours used
were produced from various earth pigments. It has not yet
been established what was the binding medium, but blood,
egg and fat have been suggested. All sorts of activities are

shown, including fights with other groups (which sometimes helps to date the painting) and even European ships
and travellers.

The rock-art shows the Bushman's view of his world,
and it is possible to see in the paintings activities which are
practised by the Kalahari Bushmen today and to appreciate
the continuity in the way of life from past to present
times. The beauty and sensitivity of the art are impressive
and further fascination lies in trying to understand its
motive, be it symbolism, magic or pleasure.

It is difficult to estimate the age of the paintings.
Recently, however, in South West Africa, some have been
found associated with cave deposits dated at about
24–26 000 years old, which is much older than had hitherto
been generally believed.

THE BUSHMEN TODAY – MODERN TRENDS

Contact with people of other cultures has brought many changes to the Bushmen, and this over a fairly long period of time. The first changes were in material things. Iron was an important early acquisition first from black neighbours and then from white. It enabled them to tip their arrow points with iron and to make useful cutting tools such as knives, adzes and axes with which to carve wood more efficiently. The pleasure of tobacco was discovered. New musical instruments were copied and other practices such as the art of divination with divining tablets were adopted. With the advent of white neighbours items of western clothing, blankets, ornaments and fire-making equipment became available, and latterly metal and plastic utensils.

More significant have been the social changes. Bushmen have frequently become the servants or serfs of other people, black and white, who have employed them especially as cattle herds, and sometimes as hunters, which introduced them to the use of guns and metal game-traps, and they have even been recruited for certain industrial work.

In some areas today, especially in Botswana and the Kavango area of South West Africa, Bushmen have started to work at other crafts, for example basketwork, wood-carving and even smithing, and to sell their wares to local people. The curio trade is encouraging a greater output of their own crafts in the making of ornaments and other objects that sell well. Christian missions and schools have been established. Government authorities are sinking bore-holes to provide permanent water and it is hoped to encourage Bushmen to settle, own cattle, plant crops and build more substantial dwellings. Thus they are gradually being drawn into the modern world. Those few Bushmen of the Kalahari who live well away from other people and maintain the old hunting and gathering way of life show, like their ancestors, a high degree of cultural adaptation to their environment. They do not over-hunt nor do they strip an area of food plants. They may at times be under-nourished but they are not malnourished. The danger of modernization in the same environment is that this adaptation may break down.